TABLE OF CONTENTS

Thank you for taking the time to look at our book! Throughout this book we will look at, talk about, and explain how you can become a successful YouTuber by utilizing Google Trends and other social media growth tips to your advantage.

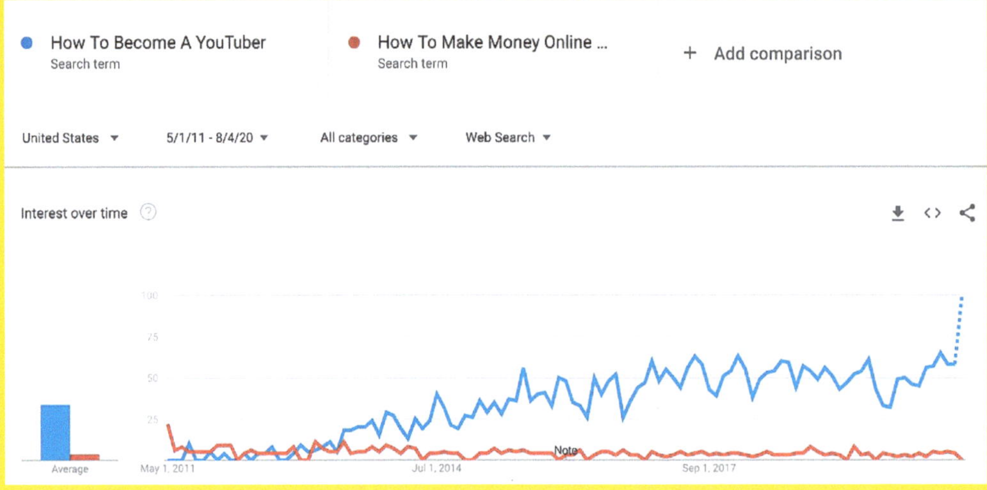

With more than a billion users in 75+ languages, YouTube connects with one-third of global internet users and provides creators and advertisers opportunities to reach large-scale audiences. Have you ever wondered how 16,000 YouTube accounts have millions of subscribers and get hundreds of thousands of views a day? Have you ever aspired and hoped that one day your YouTube channel could generate you a passive income stream? Global Social Media Marketing is here to help you do just that! In thi s ebook you'll learn the ins and outs of how to become a YouTuber!

We will break down YouTube channel growth into six chapters full of actionable strategies of information you can implement right away. These chapters cover:

1. YouTube video production equipment and skills
2. Proven strategies to successfully grow your channel
3. Optimizations and Reporting
4. YouTube content formatting
5. YouTube advertising 6. Tracking your channel with the YouTube Revenue Report

Not only do we want you to succeed and become the best YouTuber you've always wanted to be, but we want to be the ones to help you get there. You got this!

Benjamin Kepner

Benjamin Kepner, CEO of Global Social Media Marketing

ABOUT THE AUTHOR

Benjamin Kepner, Social Media Marketing Agency CEO of Global Social Media Marketing, has a decade of experience growing millions in global sales with technology, partnership marketing, digital marketing, and social media, for 80 brands and 80 events in 30 industries. He has presented YouTube presentations as a featured speaker at major education technology conferences such as Upstate Technology Conference, EdTechTeam, and AppsEvents. He has produced over 300 YouTube videos that have generated millions of views and hundreds of thousands of sales.

His YouTube marketing course has helped his many clients become more confident in their YouTube marketing skills, improved their knowledge of the YouTube algorithm, and most importantly increased their YouTube video views to drive monetization of videos for profit!

Daniel Bracey, co-author of this book, resides in Los Angeles and is pursuing a career in television writing. He's held jobs at Warner Bros., Netflix, Universal, and various animation studios. When he's not working, he wastes time on social media, writes TV pilots, and creates short films and comedic sketches.

"STOP THINKING OF 'VIDEO MARKETING' AS THIS SEPARATE ENTITY THAT IS OPTIONAL FOR YOUR BUSINESS. VIDEO IS AN EFFECTIVE FORM OF COMMUNICATION THAT NEEDS TO BE INTEGRATED INTO EACH AND EVERY ASPECT OF YOUR EXISTING MARKETING EFFORTS."

- James Wedmore, YouTube Marketer

CHAPTER 1

YouTube Video Production Equipment And Skills

Below are three of the most important things one should keep in mind when honing their YouTube video production skills. And since they all happen to start with the letter 'L', let's just call them the Three L's!

Lighting
One of the most important YouTube video production skills to have is familiarity with lighting. But for now, let's stick with some basics. If you're inside, you can use practical lights like a lamp, a simple lighting kit, or natural light from a window. These lights are good if you have limited resources or want to give your video a simple and informal vibe. A starter's lighting kit doesn't need to be fancy or expensive. Something simple like Chinese lanterns is cost-effective and great to use.

The light should always be outside the view of the camera facing you/the subject. If someone is new to video production, they won't get that having a light in the frame will cause the subject to become dark (because the camera takes in more light from the light source, rather than bouncing off the subject itself).

Listen (Audio)
Just as when you're watching a video or speaking with another person, you want to be able to hear them clearly. When the audio is too low, people have to strain to hear what you're saying, but when it's too loud it can become uncomfortable to listen to. Make sure the volume of the sound in your video is in a nice mid-range, and try to record in a quiet space without any distracting sounds. Purchasing something as simple as a shotgun microphone goes a long way and is much better than a simple microphone on your phone! In your editing software, adjust your audio input, or gain, to a nice midrange. This is arbitrary, but -12 dB to -18 dB usually works pretty well. We at Global Social media Marketing are all about Logitech and Apple Airpods.

Location
Picking the right location makes every one of the Three L's easier to achieve. The perfect location is one that's free of any distracting objects or background elements, quiet and well-lit. Unless you're recording a specific location (such as your workplace), try to record in as clear an area as possible to keep the focus on the subject of the video. With sites like Airbnb and PeerSpace at our disposal now, it's easier than ever to find that perfect location for a video! YouTube channels with 10k+ subscribers have access to YouTube Space, which offers them access to events.

Shooting
When it comes to choosing the shot you want, and executing, the lists that makeup shot tips, shot tricks, shot types are extensive and full of information. To give you some very basic ideas, three of the most common shot choices are close up, medium, and wide shots.

- A **wide shot** helps set up the scene and gives the viewer context.

- A **medium shot** is all-purpose and can offer clues or direct the focus of the user to what's coming next.

- A **close-up shot** is often used to hone in on personal, intimate conversations without distractions.

Wide Shot	Medium Shot	Close-Up

Shot composition is simply how a shot looks through the camera lens. Many mobile devices today have surprisingly high-quality cameras, so much so that TV crews have used them for impromptu clips every now and then. Your mobile device should not be your main tool but don't forget about it if you find yourself faced with a great, unexpected opportunity for a video. You can record it and upload it later or even use the YouTube app to share special clips while you're on the go.

Editing

Mac computers come with a built-in video editing program called iMovie.

YouTube Video Editor lets you combine multiple videos and images you've uploaded to create a new video. You can also trim your clips to custom lengths or add music to your video from a library of approved tracks. Be sure to customize clips with special tools and effects.

Third-party editing software is better than ever and we would recommend the following based on our experience. The most popular are Avid Media Composer and Adobe Premiere. Final Cut Pro X is more or less an upgraded version of iMovie. Screencastify is a wonderful Google Chrome extension that allows you to screen capture your display and edit it however you deem fit. It's great for tutorials and/or instructional videos.

Here is an extensive breakdown chart not only comparing Avid, Premiere, iMovie, and Final Cut, but tons of other editing software!

Video Editing (The Basics)

Trim: Cut the length of your clip by moving your cursor over the edges of your video in the timeline. Drag the handles toward the center of the video to shorten.

Lengthen: Drag the handles outward from the center of the video to lengthen. This will result in the video repeating.

Cut/Snip: Clips can be cut into portions. Move your mouse over the video and click the scissors icon to bring up the snip marker.

Here is a screengrab of using the Chrome editing extension Screencastify:

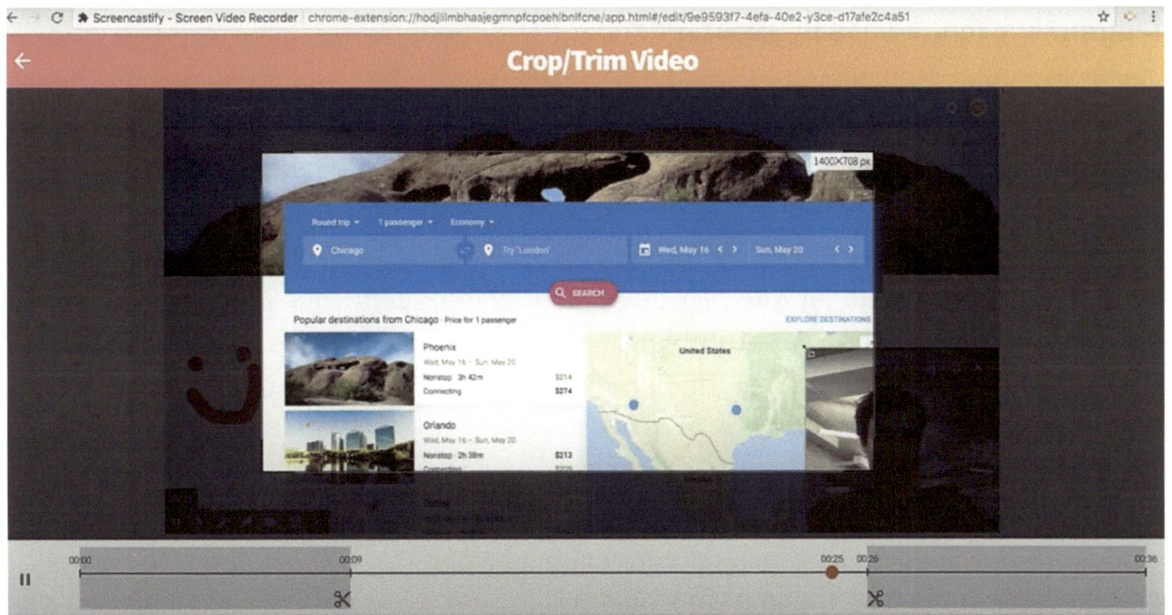

Customized YouTube Enhancements

Rotate: Rotates your video 90 degrees.
Effects: Use Video Enhancements on your video to color correct, stabilize, and add filters and other effects.
Text: Apply a text overlay on the clip.
Slow Motion: Modify the speed at which the clip plays.

Add Music And Customize The Volume

You can add a new audio track to your video. By default, the audio from an added track will replace your clips' original audio. Click the **music note** button in the upper left of the editor to bring up YouTube's library of pre-approved songs. Browse the tracks by searching or filtering by artist and genre. Some great sites to grab stock music/audio are Premium Beat, Storyblocks, and Freesound.

YouTube Ad Format

Staying up to date with YouTube ad format specifications is very important. And there's a lot to it. Check out this detailed breakdown here so you can stay informed!

Distributing Your Videos By Cross-Posting

Once your video is shot, edited, and built the way you want it, you should share/post it on your accounts and with the world! The best way to help build up your accounts on StumbleUpon/Reddit/Digg is to cross-post the top posts on each website. For example, post the top recent posts on Digg into your StumbleUpon account, post the top recent posts on StumbleUpon into your Reddit account, etc. That way you will always have fresh material with proven popularity to post in your various social media accounts! Try it out with your StumbleUpon/Reddit/Digg accounts to increase their value. You can also distribute in the Facebook groups YouTube 4,000 Watch Hours and the Help Small YouTubers Grow. These are just two examples of many!

YouTube Trailers And Descriptions

The #1 goal of a YouTube trailer video is for new visitors to understand what types of videos they can expect to watch on your channel when you will release new videos and the benefit of subscribing to the channel.

Channel Descriptions

Include the most important information, like a tagline at the beginning. Use Google Trends to identify searchable keywords to include.

When setting up your YouTube channel, make sure:

-Your channel art and text look good on smaller screens.
-Your video titles have important keywords in front so they're not cut off.
-Communicate your channel's mission statement.
-Consistent branding with your website and other channel arts.

-You create a channel trailer to help.
-You have quarterly business goals.

Channel Trailers

- Include a hook in the first 15 seconds so a majority of the audience hears it.
- Enable the channel trailer for unsubscribed viewers so that it auto-plays for them.

A screengrab from a YouTube trailer for Waste Connections of Colorado

Make sure your channel trailer focuses on your channel's mission statement.The #1 goal of a YouTube trailer video is for new visitors to understand what types of videos they can expect to watch on your channel when you will release new videos and the benefit of subscribing to the channel.A mission statement for a channel establishes the channel's purpose and guides its future decisions by communicating to your audience what content is available and why they would be interested.

Here is a breakdown on how to create a captivating YouTube trailer:

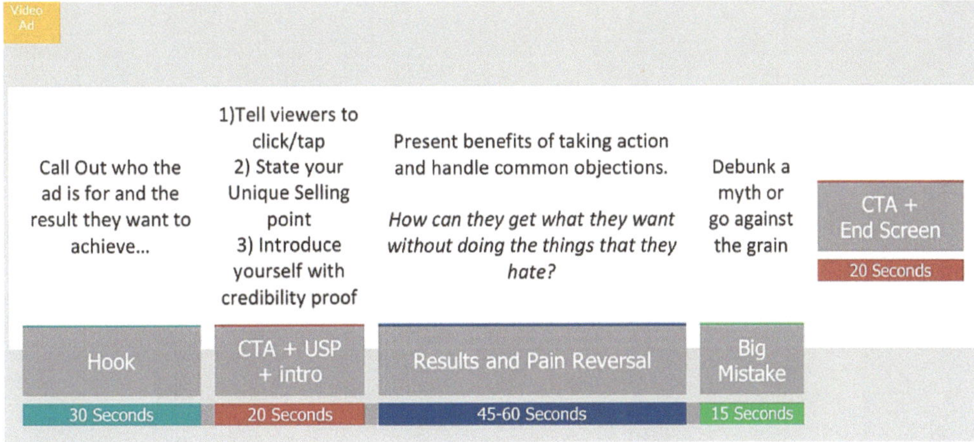

A great trailer successfully describes the channel's value proposition and summarizes the content themes. Some tips when putting together a solid mission statement while setting up your YouTube channel:

-Add the mission statement to your channel's 'About' tab.
-Set a vision for your business on YouTube.
-Optimize the channel, banner, and icon art banner only on desktop
-Check out additional areas to showcase your brand.
-Use a branding watermark to embed your channel logo.

A YouTube channel can communicate the mission and brand through its channel trailer description. These elements communicate what the channel offers as a whole, introducing viewers to the content and enticing them to watch more. The trailer and description invite viewers to subscribe, the trailer highlights the diversity of content available, and the description summarizes the video upload schedule! If need be, you can even write out a script for your trailer.

CHAPTER 2

Becoming A Successful YouTuber

When you log onto your YouTube account, do you ever see a low amount of traffic coming through your channel? Struggling to grow your YouTube subscribers? People who subscribe to channels — to any YouTube channel — are more engaged. They seek out content, comment on, share videos, and contribute to your target YouTube communities. Your subscribers are your brand evangelists. Show your most dedicated subscribers they matter to you by hearing their comments. Show them more love, pin excellent comments at the top of the feed, and shout-out your top subscribers. Now how can you convert casual viewers into more channel subscribers? In much the same way that solo creators build their followings:

- **Develop a creed**: What is your point-of-view? How might your viewers' beliefs overlap what your organization stands for?
- **Leverage a creation story:** Share your (brand's) humble beginnings to make your message more relatable.
- **Demonstrate leadership**: Use a consistent voice; most people subscribe to. personalities they like. How can your brand showcase authority or leadership?
- **Connect with rituals**: Can you include some repeated elements in your videos for fans to look forward to?
- **Create a language**: This goes beyond being conversational; special coded words or "lingo" can help viewers feel like insiders.

Ways To Get Discovered/Noticed/Grow Subscribers:

Organic: YouTube mobile app, home page, watch page, channel page, suggested video, partner promotion, cards or annotations, playlists, subscriber feed, or search.
Partner: Work with a creator or company that might be able to quickly gain credibility on YouTube. As long as the partnership works for both parties, this strategy can work well for a long-term relationship.

Paid Media: TrueView or display ads, discovery ads, banner, homepage takeover.
Goal: Make it your mission to be noticed and grow your channel! Set a plan, go above and beyond.

Viewers could also find your Youtube content on a blog/website or a notification throug social media. First, find out where people are currently watching your videos aside from YouTube, and then prioritize which blogs or platforms to target.
The subscribers reportwav in YouTube Analytics reveals the source and location of your subscribers. You can segment the data with filters ("Subscribed" and/or "Not Subscribed") to understand what they watch and how they discover your videos. You can also click "Embedded player on other websites" to determine which websites are frequently promoting your videos. These results should help inform your community and outreach efforts.

Example of a YouTube Subscribers Report

Make sure you read the YouTube Community Guidelines. Take any necessary precautions/steps to keep your channel made up of loyal subscribers. You can create a blocked words list to prevent certain words or phrases. If a user has written something inappropriate in the comments, you can remove the comment (and all of its replies) and flag the commeny for removal. Hide that user from your channel. This action blocks them from posting comments on any of your videos or contacting you through private messages. Users are not alerted when you block them.

Stick To A Schedule!

Develop rituals for communicating the upload schedule, video formats, and special events. Adopt special lingo for code words or specific language on your channel.

Examples from the Global Social Media Marketing channel include: wave spell, instantly, the unquestionable supremacy of nature, just gonna send it, family, let's get cheesy, reindeer gang, bash brothers, hula crew, etc.

Video Inspiration!

One way to grow your YouTube community is by producing a channel trailer that tells the story of your journey leading up to YouTube. What moments during your videos does your community anticipate? Repeat a similar greeting in each video to establish a ritual. Try to be the first to comment on each video you upload. Make a habit of responding to comments in the first few hours after uploading a new video. Share links to relevant videos and photos to boost engagement. If you're not in front of a desktop computer, you can use the YouTube Studio App.

Conversation, Comments, And Care!

Select what your audience sees first to help set the tone of the conversation by pinning comments at the top of the feed. Viewers will also be notified if you pin their comments (and they opt into notifications). This can encourage fan contributions. Highlight the answer to a common question or add a heart that will send a notification to the viewer who wrote the comment. Viewers who have received a heart on their comments are three times more likely to click on the notification (than with other types of notifications), potentially leading more viewers back to your channel. Hearts are different from 'Likes'. Only YouTube creators have access to hearts, whereas, viewers and creators can click like or dislike next to a comment. With highlighted usernames, it's easier than ever to see your replies because the channel creator's username will be highlighted. Viewers see you're present and care!

Comments from a GSMM video

↑ Pinned by Global Social Media Marketing
Butterfly Simmer 4 months ago
Anyone else using google hangouts for their online classes XD? thanks for the video

👍 29 👎 💬 **REPLY**
▼ View 3 replies from Global Social Media Marketing and others

200 Subs with 0 Videos challenge 3 months ago
Coronavirus: shuts down schools
Video: views skyrocket

👍 5 👎 💬 **REPLY**
▼ View reply from Global Social Media Marketing

free energy 3 months ago
damn get to the point never wanted to got to college ...to much bull

👍 2 👎 💬 **REPLY**
▼ View reply from Global Social Media Marketing

M C 4 months ago
Thank you so much for this tutorial!!

👍 1 👎 💬 **REPLY**
▼ View reply from Global Social Media Marketing

Barbara Morgan 4 months ago
Thanks. I need to practice using this now.

👍 5 👎 💬 **REPLY**
▼ View reply from Global Social Media Marketing

Jacqueline Jackson 6 months ago
Thank you for the video. very informative. Can it be used with a guest who does not have a gmail account?

👍 3 👎 💬 **REPLY**
▼ View 3 replies from Global Social Media Marketing and others

The Proof Architect 4 months ago
Hi thank you for the video. This is very good for scheduled calls. I'm even having trouble started trying to invite someone to join my Google Hangouts contact list in the first place. Do you know how to do that? Thank you.

Promote With Hashtags!

Share hashtags(#) in your videos and consider asking your audience to create content around these topics. Make videos about your community. Fans love to see when a channel they're dedicated to makes a video for them. Consider producing a thank you video for your audience or to celebrate milestones. Recognize your most loyal viewers, and show them how much you appreciate them! If you ask your viewers to submit comments or answer questions, consider featuring their replies in your next video. Seeing their comments or usernames can inspire your community to interact even more. Hosting live streams to reward top community members is a great way to interact as well.

YT Membership

$4.99/month

JOIN

Recurring payment. Cancel anytime. Creator may update perks from time to time.

Loyalty badges next to your name in comments and live chat

Custom emoji to use in live chat

Exclusive "Sponsor Only" Q&A Live Streams
Each month we will be going in-depth with sponsor only Q&A Live streams.

Access to Private Speaking Replays
Get exclusive replay access to my speaking new private YouTube presentations

Get Access to Private Discord Group
As a member you get access to Derral's private discord group (Channel Jumpstart).

Short list of In-depth Channel Evaluations
Be on the list the short list of channels that Derral will pick for his Channel Reviews.

Your name (Global Social Media Marketing) and member status may be publicly visible and shared by the channel with 3rd parties (to provide perks). Learn more

Watch Time Is important!

Watch time measures how engaged viewers are with what they're watching and growing with your channel. Why is this metric so important? Your content benefits when it leads viewers to spend more time watching videos. Not just on your channel, but anywhere on YouTube. Watch time is measured in cumulative minutes watched, and each video uploaded. Every channel on YouTube is "ranked" by watch time. Channels and videos with higher watch times are likely to show up higher in search results and recommendations. The average length of the top ads that made YouTube's 2019 year-end leaderboard was about thirty seconds. Watch time benefits don't evaporate when viewers stop watching your content.

The total amount of time a viewer spends on YouTube in a single visit is called a watch session. If a video on your brand's channel drives them to watch more videos, the channel earns some watch time credits for the cumulative minutes accrued.

Use "Related Videos" To Your Advantage!

What videos, YouTubers, Brands, or Personalities would you want to be associated with? One huge way to get traffic on YouTube is by showing up in the related videos. Create videos with similar titles and keywords to the videos you want to be associated with. Quote the person or brand and use their name in the title and keywords. Consider interviewing or collaborating with them to increase the association in YouTube's eyes.

CHAPTER 3

YouTube Growth Tips

What To Ask When Conducting A Channel Assessment:

-What content should we promote/produce?
-Which content is getting watched the most?

-Which content best keeps viewers' attention?
-How do we maximize viewership?
-How do we get our content discovered and build loyalty?
-How do we reach an international audience?
-How do we best enrich our content with interactivity?

When it comes to a successful upswing in YouTube Channel Growth, launching a YouTube channel is when an audience analysis typically happens. Identify which audience fits with the mission, brand, and content strategy. After a channel is up and running, it's valuable to assess whether the actual audience matches the target.

Show them first hand what you have to offer by sharing useful information, how-to guides and sneak peeks, issuing calls-to-action, and simply communicating with them either in the comments or YouTube inbox messages.

Collect and analyze that data. You may need to measure several dimensions to validate. Look at the overall number of subscribers gained, then use the multi-line view to identify watch time impact by video.

Identify if a change is needed and implement solutions based on the analysis. Your implementation plan typically would reflect which improvements can yield the best possible results. If your latest video series is gaining fewer subscribers, check the verbal and visual calls to action and your mission statement. While mission statements vary in style, you can check yours against these recommendations:

- Describe the channel's value proposition
- Summarize the content themes
- Identify the target audience
- Tell your channel's story about its mission and brand through its channel trailer and channel description (About tab). When a channel reaches 100,000 subscribers, it can submit a request to YouTube for a verification badge.

Assess Content Strategy

People usually come to YouTube to be entertained, educated, or inspired. Content that targets viewer intentions can drive stronger audience engagement. Videos satisfying these needs are more likely to keep interest up.

Avoid Dips And Declines

Dips (red arrows) mean viewers are skipping over those parts of the video. Eliminate or shorten elements that consistently result in dips and declines. A sudden drop (red arrow) means viewers are leaving the video within the first few seconds. This usually indicates the video didn't match the viewers' expectations.

Ensure that the title, thumbnail, and description reflect the content. If one type of content gets a higher percentage of dislikes than others, consider whether it covers a controversial topic or diverges from the usual topics featured on the channel.

Comments can help you figure out subjects that appeal to the audience so the channel can create more videos on those subjects. You can even drill deeper into interesting sources of traffic. For example, within YouTube search, you can look at the top 25 keywords that people search for to find your videos, which can help you to optimize video metadata for what viewers are searching for.

Subscribers are key to a YouTube channel's growth success. They help drive views up on the first day of the upload, contributing to increased discovery by non-subscribers.

If the largest traffic source is external, that may present an opportunity for partnering with one of those websites to drive even more traffic to the channel. Also, when you see a large spike or drop in a traffic source, you can investigate the potential cause. Some channels enable optional tabs or buttons in their social media feeds to link to YouTube. YouTube uses video metadata (titles, tags, and descriptions) to index videos against viewer searches. By optimizing metadata, a channel can maximize its presence in YouTube search, promotion, suggested videos, and ad-serving.

To determine if a channel has effective metadata, you can evaluate whether:

- Video titles, tags, and description accurately represent the content
- Video titles have the most important keywords in front so they're not cut off
- Video tags are listed in order of relevance to the video
- Video descriptions are searchable and understandable

What Is Your YouTube Channel's Growth Global Reach?

YouTube is available in 60+ different languages, covering 95% of the Internet population. Overall, 80% of YouTube's views are from outside the U.S. You can make it easier for international viewers to find a channel, and improve the viewing experience, with captions, subtitles, and translated metadata. To evaluate your YouTube channel's growing global reach, first, look at the Watch Time report, then examine "watch time per country – share by viewers". You can measure where views are coming from by country, comparing subscribers and non-subscribers. With this, identify countries where a channel can improve discovery.

Subtitles are translations of captions. They offer audiences who do not speak the same language as well as people who are hearing impaired. You can translate and write subtitles yourself or crowdsource them from your community by enabling "Community Contributions".

What's more, individuals, media companies, and brands alike can own channels and create content for YouTube! High quality monetized content, engaged viewers, and high traffic help fuel the ecosystem with advertising dollars. Enabling monetization funds the channel owner and provides an opportunity for advertisers and brands to reach audiences with on-demand relevant content.

Here is a quick breakdown of how much a YouTuber can make:

-YouTubers earn between 0.3 cents to 1 cent per view.
-Youtubers don't get paid per subscriber, but subscribers are the ones who are most likely to watch your videos.
-Every 1,000 views a YouTuber can make anywhere between $3 and $10, although that can be higher or lower in some cases.
-How much a YouTuber makes per video depends on viewership and the ads displayed by Google, but it could be loads. For example, if a video has 1 million views, a YouTuber could be cashing anything between $3,000 and $10,000!
-When you reach the balance goal of $100 YouTube will pay you.

-Channels also have the opportunity to earn revenue off YouTube by:

1. Selling merchandise and/or crowdfunding through approved third-party retailers.

2. Getting paid sponsorships.

3. Collaborating with brands to produce branded content.

Advertisers target ad placement based on the audience demographics, the geographic location of viewers, and device viewers are watching on. Check the channel's studio to see if the audience of your channel could match with potential brands (target audience behaviors and interests) and to see which ad formats are enabled on the devices your viewers are watching. Since advertisers can specify certain viewer demographics when they bid on an ad (e.g. age, gender, geography, content category).

The demographic and behavioral attributes of a viewer can influence the ad serving model. The model checks to see if the ad type can display on the viewer's device (some ads may not display on mobile), whether the video is embedded, if the viewer is a YouTube Premium subscriber, and if a viewer has just seen an ad. 85% of adults ages 18-49 use multiple devices at the same time and two-thirds watch YouTube on a second screen while watching TV at home. What makes YouTube unique is that the platform breaks down the fourth wall and invites viewers to take part in an interactive viewing experience anytime, anywhere, across multiple screens.

Over 400 hours of content are uploaded onto YouTube for education, entertainment, and inspire viewers. YouTube reaches over one billion unique viewers globally who watch over six billion hours of YouTube videos each month! And they aren't just passively watching content. They're constantly engaging with channels.

Micro-moments occur when people reflexively turn to a device—increasingly a smartphone—to act on a need to learn something, do something, discover something, watch something, or buy something.

Promote Your Channel

Improving the quality of your videos will be an ongoing process, so make notes for what you can do in future videos. Link to or embed your videos on your websites. Submit to other websites and blogs. You should also create and maintain a list of different blogs or online directories where you submit your videos.

You can grab links to share your video by clicking the share tab beneath a public video and either share it directly from a network or grab the URL or embed code. Utilize your social network and let your audience know that they are free to share your videos. Word-of-mouth is always fantastic.

How To Best Grow Your Viewership

1. **Maximizing Viewership:** How many views (or how much watch time) do we have? What content is causing changes?
2. **Promoting/producing Content:** Which content elicits a favorable reaction? Which content is getting watched the most? Which content best keeps viewers' attention? Who/where are my viewers?
3. **Making our Content More Discoverable:** How do people find our content? How do people watch our content? When should we upload content?
4. **Building Loyalty:** How many people have subscribed? How loyal are viewers? How loyal are subscribers?
5. **Reaching an International Audience:** Which other languages should we target? How many views benefit from captions?
6. **Enriching our Content With Interactivity:** How do cards and end screens perform?

There are three important parties when it comes to a successful YouTube video:

- **Viewers –** Want to be entertained, learn, and join an interactive community. They make up the diverse audience of YouTube that brands and creators want to reach.
- **Creators –** They express themselves, share their creativity, and those with great content and engaged viewers can build a business with their YouTube channel.
- **Advertisers –** Creators use these as a way to reach and target their audiences. Advertisers purchase ads with specific demographics.

CHAPTER 4

YouTube Legal Practices

Improving your YouTube content ownership knowledge is crucial, and it all boils down to copyright. Copyright is just one form of intellectual property law that protects original works of authorship for a set period of time. If you're the copyright owner, this protection grants you exclusive rights to control how your work is used and who can make money from it. In the United States, copyright registration (with the U.S. Copyright Office) may be necessary before filing an infringement suit. In other jurisdictions, a copyright registration may not be available or may provide more limited benefits. Remember, copyright law is national, so get local advice. When it comes to YouTube content ownership and its creation, these videos are subject to copyright protection the moment they're created, not based upon who is the first to register or upload them.

Copyright Protects:

- Sound recordings and musical compositions
- Written works, such as lectures, articles, and books
- Visual works, such as photos, paintings, posters, and ads
- Video games and computer software
- Dramatic works, such as plays and musicals

Privacy Is Important!

If someone posts a video of you without your consent, you may request removal if you're uniquely identifiable by image, voice, full name, or other personal information. This is separate from a copyright complaint. YouTube also has policies to handle other situations, such as harassment and harmful content. To find out more, visit YouTube's Policy and Safety Hub and review our Community Guidelines.

What You Are Able To Do:

-Trademark complaint: A video improperly uses our brand name or distinctive mark.
-Privacy complaint: I appear in this video without my consent
-Reporting tool: Someone is maliciously attacking me online
-Flagging tool: I found a video that incites violence or dangerous activity

Spot When You Need Copyright Permissions And Licenses

When it comes to YouTube content ownership, you must secure the rights to all elements in your video—including any music (also background music), video clips, photos, etc. The first step would be to contact the copyright owners or rights-holders directly and negotiate the appropriate licenses. Licenses typically contain explicit permission for using the content but may include limitations on exclusivity, specific rights, duration, geography, or other terms. You should seek legal advice for any licensing agreement to be certain which rights are granted and which rights are reserved by the owner.

A Creative Commons license (CC-BY license) provides different kinds of open licenses so content owners can grant someone else permission to use their work under certain circumstances. Over four million Creative Commons licensed videos are on YouTube. Anyone can remix, transform, and build upon the material in these videos for free.

Be Smart On Your Phone!

Just because you record something on your smartphone or other device doesn't mean you automatically own the copyright for what it contains. For example, if you record concert footage, the rights to the material could be held by the performer, music label, and publisher. Even if you purchase content, such as a song from iTunes/Apple Music, you don't inherently have the right to use that content.

Some people assume making a cover song doesn't require a license. If you perform a cover song, make sure you have permission from the copyright owners. You may need additional licenses to reproduce the original sound recording, including the song in a video, or display the lyrics. A less convoluted way to help creators find music is the YouTube Audio Library. It offers free music and sound effects, which can be used in videos according to the terms specified.

Use Works Fairly With Fair Use

Fair use (or fair dealing) is a legal doctrine and defense that says you can reuse copyright-protected material under certain circumstances without getting permission from the copyright owner. Courts have ruled that rights holders must consider fair use or fair dealing before they send a copyright takedown notice. Courts will analyze a specific case based on a set of principles to consider whether a piece of content can benefit from fair use or fair dealing exceptions. For example, works of commentary, criticism, research, teaching, or news reporting might be considered fair use or dealing.

Specific rules relating to fair use or fair dealing vary on a national basis. By way of example when analyzing a specific case, U.S. courts look at the four factors of fair use:

-The purpose and character of the use, including whether such use is commercial is for nonprofit educational purposes
-The nature of the copyrighted work
-The amount and substantiality of the portion used in relation to the copyrighted work as a whole
-The effect of the use upon the potential market for or value of, the copyrighted work

Giving credit to the copyright owner or including a disclaimer such as "no infringement intended" doesn't necessarily constitute fair use. Similarly, declaring an upload to be "for entertainment purposes only" isn't an automatic defense. Even if you add original content to someone's copyrighted work, your video may not qualify as fair use, so be sure to carefully consider all four factors and get legal advice if needed. For example, a video could make use of existing content in a new and transformative way that has social value beyond the original, such as a parody or critique.

Access The Public Domain

Copyright protects works for a set period of time. The length of a term of copyright protection depends on various factors, such as the date and place of publication and whether it's a work of corporate authorship. When works eventually lose their copyright protection, they fall into the "public domain," making them free for everyone. There's no official list of works in the public domain, so it will be your responsibility to verify that a work is in the public domain if you want to use it.

CHAPTER 5

YouTube Ads

Video ads run on YouTube and across the web through the Google Display Network. With more than one billion users, YouTube is available in 70+ countries and 60+ languages and offers rich content from all over the world. The Display Network reaches over 90% of Internet users through two million sites and apps (source: Comscore). By creating effective ads, you can advertise to consumers at moments that matter. When advertising to obtain the correct audience, you must keep in mind:

Demographic Groups: Choose the age, gender, parental status, or household income of the audience you want to reach.

Interests: Pick from available audience categories to reach people interested in certain topics, even when they may be visiting pages about other topics.

Affinity Audiences: Raise brand awareness and drive consideration with your video ads by reaching people who already have a strong interest in relevant topics.

Custom Affinity Audiences: Create audiences that are more tailored to your brands, compared to our broad, TV-like affinity audiences. For example, rather than reaching sports fans, a running shoe company may want to reach avid marathon runners instead. Or try to reach people who have recently experienced a major change in lifestyle or people based on their consumption habits, such as where they shop or eat.

Research what is "in" and trending to keep up with your competitors! Find the most-used apps and most-visited sites.

In-Market Audiences: Find customers who are researching products and actively considering buying a service or product like those you offer. Some of these In-Market Audiences are: Apparel and Accessories, Business Services, and Dating Services.

Video Remarketing: Reach viewers based on their past interactions with your videos, TrueView ads, or YouTube channel. If you've linked your YouTube account to your Ads account already, we'll create custom lists for you automatically. Learn more about remarketing lists for YouTube viewers.

Different Types of Ads

Standard In-Stream: This is a non-skippable format that plays before a video. It's ideal if you want to communicate a simple, powerful message and get visibility. It forces the impression and won't accrue views on the video. Standard in-stream ads can be a maximum of 15 or 30 seconds. Those that are a maximum of 30 seconds can run only on long-form videos (10 minutes or longer). When you click on a video at the top of YouTube search results, you will see an ad at the beginning of the video you can skip - this is the TrueView in-stream ad. You can place these ads on any YouTube channel, the most-watched leadership training videos, and other websites. You only get charged if they watch 30 seconds of the video and if they don't you get FREE exposure. You can also retarget views once we have over 1,000+. There is also a 1/3 of the competition on YouTube compared to Facebook and people go to YouTube to get educated ("How to" learn or do something) A good YouTube lead ad is 1:44-3:00 in length and uses the following practice of **Grab -> Teach -> Invite**:

Grab: Their attention in the first 5 seconds with something visually stunning or outrageous; Billy Gene Marketing is the master of this if you watch a few of his videos)

Teach: Remind them of their pain points and teach them how you can solve them with your product or service.

Invite: Drive them to receive a value offer via an ebook, webinar, landing page, etc.

John Prendergast, an American human rights and anti-corruption activist, author, and former Director for African Affairs at the National Security Council is currently using this method for his YouTube Ads Academy.

In-Stream Select: This skippable ad appears when someone starts a video (pre-roll). It can be up to 60 seconds long, and it's skippable after 5 seconds. This format increments the view count on the YouTube video ad. Whether or not the ad is skipped, the advertiser pays on a CPM basis. Learn more about in-stream video ads.

Desktop Custom Masthead: This is a 970 x 250 pixel, an in-page unit that spans the full width of the YouTube homepage below the navigation bar. This unit, which can include a video, can drive brand relevant activity and an increase in branded search.

Desktop Universal Video Mastheads: This is a 780 x 195 that runs on the YouTube homepage. It includes a video on one side and an information panel or a flash/image panel on the other. The flash/image panel can optionally expand/close when someone clicks on/closes it.

Mobile Video Mastheads: Appears on the homepage of all YouTube mobile and tablet properties, including the Android native mobile app, the iOS app, and m.youtube.com for smartphones and tablets. It features a video thumbnail, channel icon, and customizable headline and description.

This could be your ad!

When advertising on YouTube, you can also reserve ads! A reservation campaign has a minimum spending requirement. Advertisers booking Masthead ads are encouraged to participate in a kick-off call with our technical team to get specs, turnaround times, and campaign expectations. Our advertising team sends weekly campaign performance reports for your review. You can then request targeting changes to help improve ad performance. Where you want your ads showing up is very important! To help regulate that, there are content targeting methods. These let you define where you want your ads to show. These include:

Placements: Target unique channels, videos, apps, websites, or placements within websites. For example, you can target an entire high traffic blog or just the homepage of a popular news site. Placements can include YouTube channels, YouTube videos, Websites on the Display Network, and Apps on the Display Network.

Topics: Target your video ads to specific topics on YouTube and the Display Network. Topic targeting lets you reach a broad range of videos, channels, and websites related to the topics you select.

Keywords: Depending on your video ad format, you can show your video ads based on words or phrases—keywords—related to a YouTube video, YouTube channel, or type of website.

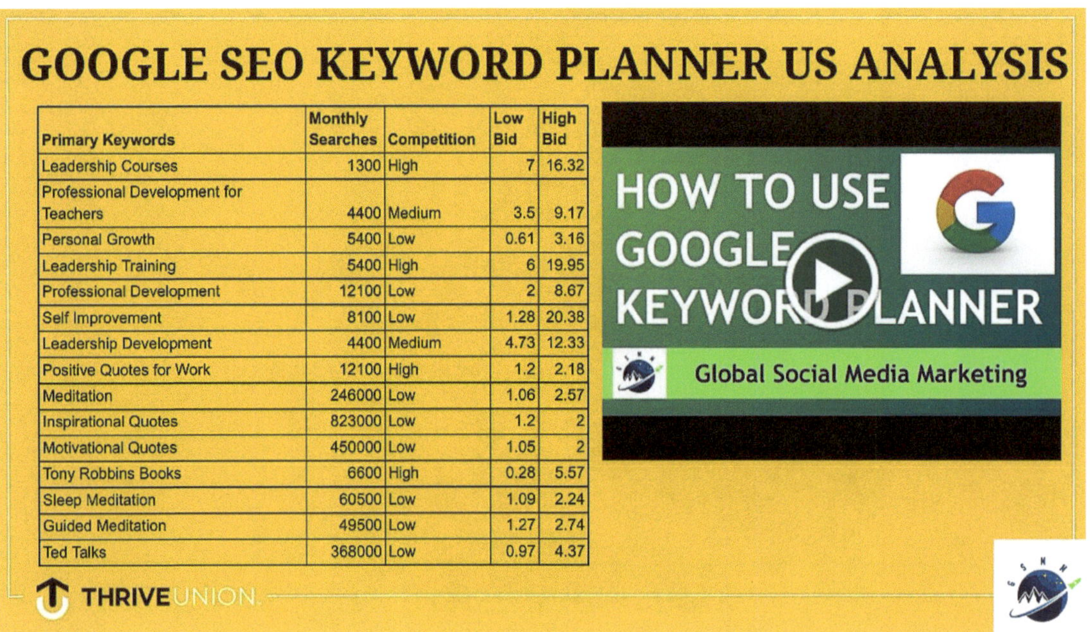

GOOGLE SEO KEYWORD PLANNER US ANALYSIS

Primary Keywords	Monthly Searches	Competition	Low Bid	High Bid
Leadership Courses	1300	High	7	16.32
Professional Development for Teachers	4400	Medium	3.5	9.17
Personal Growth	5400	Low	0.61	3.16
Leadership Training	5400	High	6	19.95
Professional Development	12100	Low	2	8.67
Self Improvement	8100	Low	1.28	20.38
Leadership Development	4400	Medium	4.73	12.33
Positive Quotes for Work	12100	High	1.2	2.18
Meditation	246000	Low	1.06	2.57
Inspirational Quotes	823000	Low	1.2	2
Motivational Quotes	450000	Low	1.05	2
Tony Robbins Books	6600	High	0.28	5.57
Sleep Meditation	60500	Low	1.09	2.24
Guided Meditation	49500	Low	1.27	2.74
Ted Talks	368000	Low	0.97	4.37

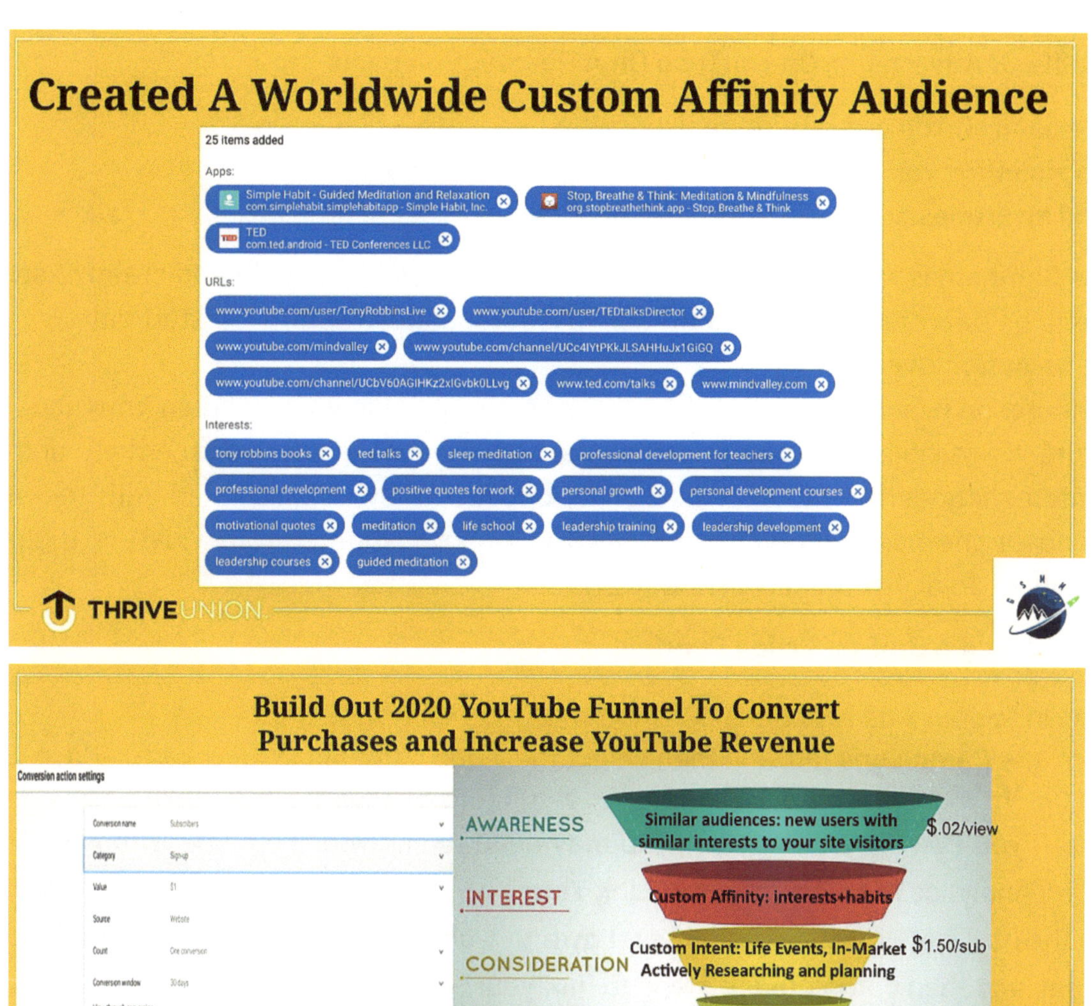

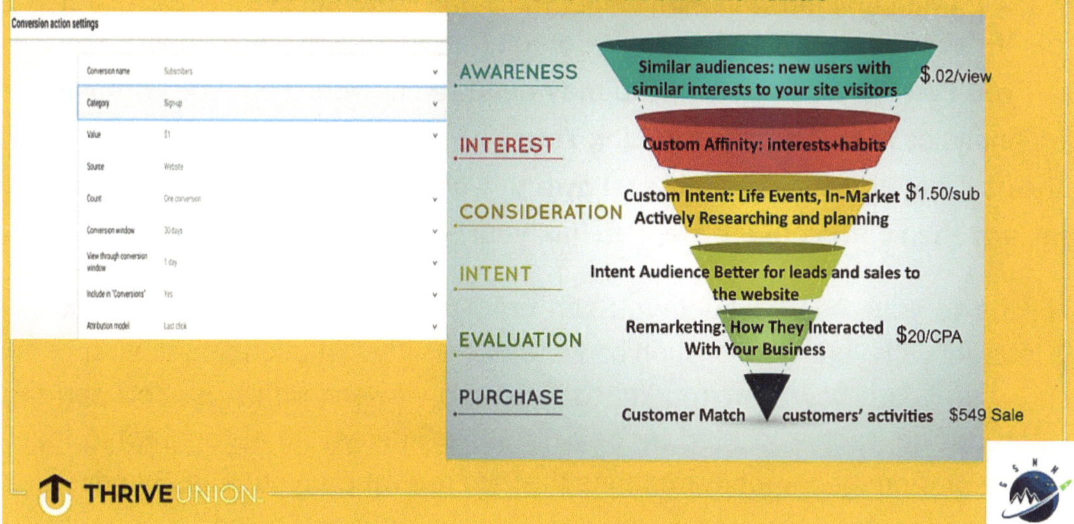

Buying Reservation Advertising

Advertisers and agencies can buy reservation advertising on a fixed, cost-per-thousand-impressions (CPM) or fixed cost-per-day (CPD) basis.

Benefits Of Advertising On YouTube On A Reservation Basis

More control: You can buy impressions at a fixed rate.
High visibility: You can run ads on the YouTube homepage.
Brand awareness: You can reach a wide audience.

CPM Campaigns have to be booked six business days in advance and creative assets need to be delivered for implementation at least four days before the start date.

Call-to-Action Overlays

Call-to-action overlays are eligible to show on any TrueView video ad on YouTube. This feature is available at no extra cost to you, can increase viewer engagement, and add an interesting element to your ads. Also, because they're associated with the video instead of the ad, call-to-action overlays will show whether your video is triggered through an ad or an organic (unpaid) view.

Steps To Add A Call-to-Action Overlay:

1. Sign in to your Ads account.
2. Click the **Campaigns** tab, and then select the video campaign you want to edit.
3. On the **Videos** tab, click **Edit Call to Action** on the "Analytics" drop-down.
       -If you don't see this option, you may need to link your YouTube with your Ads. On the "Analytics" drop-down, click "**Link Your YouTube Channel**."
4. On the box that opens, select either **I own this channel** or **Someone else owns this channel, and then complete the steps to link your account.**

After linking to your Ads account, you can create these lists based on various ways people interact with your videos, such as watching a video, subscribing to your channel, or even liking. Learn how to re-market to YouTube viewers with Ads. You can target your video ads to people located in, or who show interest in, a geographic location. Choose one or more geographic locations that are relevant to your ads. By advertising to the right customers, you can hopefully increase your return on investment (ROI). Understand that users come to YouTube to learn, watch, and be entertained. As such, create videos that feature original content!

Monetization And YouTube Analytics

The Revenue Report

By keeping track of your Revenue Report, it will show you how well you're monetizing your YouTube videos and where those revenue streams are coming from. Join the YouTube Partner Program by having 1,000 subscribers and 4,000 watch hours in the previous twelve-month period in order to be eligible. With this power, you can enable all ad formats to make sure you're eligible for all types of ad revenue. You also may be eligible to earn money from Super Chats in your live streams. Also, make sure you keep this checklist handy:

-The Revenue Report gives you an overview of the different types of revenue streams, including estimated ad revenue and estimated revenue from YouTube Premium.
-The Ads Rates Report gives you a detailed breakdown of how much money each type of ad is bringing into your channel. You can also look at how many ads play against your videos broken out by ad types. Compare the metric "Estimated Monetized Playbacks" and look for videos where views are disproportionately higher than monetized YouTube video playbacks.

This shows an overview of the different ways you can earn revenue, including net estimated revenue from ads and YouTube Premium. YouTube Premium revenue is calculated based on how much time Premium users spend with your content.

While in Creator Studio, click the video manager. Enable YouTube video monetization and check for any copyright claims against your videos. Click 'Copyright Notices' under Video Manager to see if that is the case. You can also see if your earnings have shifted geographically. Display the geographies tab in the Revenue Report and select the multi-line view to compare your revenue by country at a glance. First, enable all ad formats, especially skippable video ads (TrueView) and sponsored cards. Those ad formats are available on mobile devices, as well as computers. Focus on audience development to keep growing your fan base.

In addition to traditional creative, media, and production teams, this new landscape will demand data analysts, social media strategists, distribution experts, and YouTube experts in the space. YouTube leads in the online video space: Global users spend six billion hours watching YouTube each month, on hundreds of millions of devices! That number is insane! Because of this high number, YouTube creators must actively listen to their audience and to include viewers in creative decision making.

If you listen to your audience your viewership and subscriptions will go up, and in turn, can help monetize your channel and videos. Since everyone is trying to monetize their YouTube videos and channels, you have to think outside the box to achieve your goals.

FREE 30 MINUTE CONSULTATION!!

We hope you enjoyed reading our ebook! We at GSMM would love to go more in-depth with you about our YouTube success process.

But if growing your YouTube isn't your cup of tea, that's okay! We also offer growth courses in the many other realms of social media. Head to
www.globalsocialmediamarketing.com

to schedule a thirty-minute chat with our CEO Benjamin Kepner!